Dear Parents and Educators,

Welcome to Penguin Young Readers! As parents and educators, you know that each child develops at his or her own pace—in terms of speech, critical thinking, and, of course, reading. Penguin Young Readers recognizes this fact. As a result, each Penguin Young Readers book is assigned a traditional easy-to-read level (1–4) as well as a Guided Reading Level (A–P). Both of these systems will help you choose the right book for your child. Please refer to the back of each book for specific leveling information. Penguin Young Readers features esteemed authors and illustrators, stories about favorite characters, fascinating nonfiction, and more!

Pup-Pup-Puppies

LEVEL 2
GUIDED READING LEVEL **H**

This book is perfect for a **Progressing Reader** who:
- can figure out unknown words by using picture and context clues;
- can recognize beginning, middle, and ending sounds;
- can make and confirm predictions about what will happen in the text; and
- can distinguish between fiction and nonfiction.

Here are some **activities** you can do during and after reading this book:
- Nonfiction: Nonfiction books deal with facts and events that are real. Talk about the elements of nonfiction in this book. On a separate sheet of paper, write down what you learned about puppies.
- Make Connections: In this book, you learn how to take good care of a puppy. If you had a puppy, how would you take care of it? If you do have a puppy, what is the most important part of caring for your puppy?

Remember, sharing the love of reading with a child is the best gift you can give!

—Bonnie Bader, EdM
　　Penguin Young Readers program

*Penguin Young Readers are leveled by independent reviewers applying the standards developed by Irene Fountas
and Gay Su Pinnell in *Matching Books to Readers: Using Leveled Books in Guided Reading*, Heinemann, 1999.

To Bailey, the cutest puppy ever!—BB

PENGUIN YOUNG READERS
Published by the Penguin Group
Penguin Group (USA) LLC, 375 Hudson Street, New York, New York 10014, USA

USA | Canada | UK | Ireland | Australia | New Zealand | India | South Africa | China

penguin.com
A Penguin Random House Company

Photo credits: cover: © Mitsuaki Iwago/Minden Pictures/Corbis; page 5, page 6 (left), page 6 (right), page 7 (bottom), page 8, page 9, page 10, page 11 (bottom), page 12 (bottom), page 13 (top), page 13 (bottom), page 14 (top), page 16 (left), page 16 (right), page 17 (left), page 17 (right), page 19, page 21, page 22, page 23, page 25, page 26–27, page 28 (top), page 28 (bottom), page 32: © iStockphoto/Thinkstock/Getty Images; page 4: © Hemera/Thinkstock/Getty Images; page 7 (top), page 14–15 (bottom): © Fuse/Thinkstock/Getty Images; page 11 (top): © Gerard Brown/Dorling Kindersley/Getty Images; page 12 (top): © Neo Vision/amana images/Getty Images; page 15 (top): © Teresa Short/Flickr Open/Getty Images; page 18: © LWA/Photographer's Choice/Getty Images; page 20: © PhotoAlto/Odilon Dimier/PhotoAlto Agency RF Collections/Getty Images; page 24: © PapaGraphics/A.collection/amana images/Getty Images; page 29: © Michelle McMahon/Flickr/Getty Images; page 30: © Cindy Singleton/E+/Getty Images; page 31: © Stuart Pearce/age fotostock/Getty Images.

Text copyright © 2014 by Bonnie Bader. All rights reserved. Published by Penguin Young Readers, an imprint of Penguin Group (USA) LLC, 345 Hudson Street, New York, New York 10014. Manufactured in China.

Library of Congress Cataloging-in-Publication Data is available.

ISBN 978-0-448-47995-8 (pbk)   10 9 8 7 6 5 4 3 2
ISBN 978-0-448-47996-5 (hc)   10 9 8 7 6 5 4 3 2 1

Pup-Pup-**Puppies**

by Bonnie Bader

Penguin Young Readers
An Imprint of Penguin Group (USA) LLC

Pup.

Pup.

Puppies!

Puppies run.

Puppies jump.

Puppies like to eat some treats.

Puppies lick.

Puppies bark.

Puppies cuddle up to sleep.

Puppies make the best pets.

But not all puppies are the same.

Some puppies are small.

Some puppies are big.

Some puppies have short tails.

Some puppies have long tails.

Big or small, short or long,

all puppies are cute.

It is fun to get a new puppy.

But a new puppy is a lot of work.

A grown-up can show you

how to take good care

of your new puppy.

Do not grab your puppy.

Let your new puppy come to you.

Pet your puppy.

Pet your puppy gently.

You can teach your puppy to sit.

You can teach your puppy to stay.

Sometimes your puppy

will act badly.

You can teach your puppy

not to bite.

You can teach your puppy

not to chew.

You can teach your puppy

where to pee.

You can teach your puppy
where to sleep.

Puppies love to roll in the mud.

Bath time!

It is important to give your
puppy a bath, so that it stays
nice and clean.

Puppies always love to eat.

Dinnertime!

It is important to feed your

puppy, so that it grows big and

strong—like you!

Puppies love to go for walks.

It is important to give your puppy
lots of time outside.

You have to play with your puppy.

Park time!

You will love your puppy.

And your puppy will love you.